First published in the United States of America in 2015 by Jared A. Zichek, 2750 Torrey Pines Rd, La Jolla, California 92037, USA
E-mail: editor@retromechanix.com

ISBN: 978-0-692-50433-8

www.retromechanix.com

Front Cover: Contemporary artist's impression of the Goodyear GA-28B convoy fighter of 1950. Below this is a speculative color profile of the same aircraft in the overall Glossy Sea Blue scheme which was standard at the time it was proposed.

Back Cover: Additional speculative color profiles of the GA-28A/B, including variants with the wing pods deleted.

1) Cover to the GA-28A proposal, a three-quarter scale prototype of the GA-28B, which is in the front. Note the evolution of the configuration as the aircraft approaches the viewer.

REPORT NO. GER 2401

DATE: 20 NOVEMBER 1950

PROPOSAL
GA-28A
TRANSITION TRAINING AND RESEARCH AIRPLANE

PREPARED BY:

APPROVED BY:

GA-28A

GA-28B

▲ 1

Introduction

In the late 1940s, the US Navy Bureau of Aeronautics (BuAer) began to seriously examine the feasibility of developing a vertical takeoff and landing (VTOL) tailsitter aircraft to protect convoys, task forces, and other vessels. These specialized interceptors would be placed on the decks of ships to provide a rapid defensive and reconnaissance capability until other fighters could arrive and assist. The Battle of the Atlantic was fresh in the minds of Navy planners, who were concerned that the Soviets would engage in a similar campaign against merchant shipping if the nascent Cold War erupted into open conflict. BuAer's interest in a VTOL tailsitter fighter coincided with the development of new turboprop engines which provided enough horsepower to make the concept a reality.

In 1950, BuAer drew up Outline Specification 122 (OS-122), which listed the requirements for such an aircraft (referred to as a "convoy fighter") along with a three-quarter scale demonstrator to verify the soundness of the concept. The document was distributed to the major aircraft manufacturers of the day; of them, Convair, Goodyear, Lockheed, Martin, and Northrop submitted formal proposals on November 20, 1950. Contracts were awarded in May 1951 to Convair and Lockheed, who built the XFY-1 *Pogo* and XFV-1 *Salmon*, respectively. As many aviation enthusiasts know, these aircraft never made it beyond the prototype stage, as they proved to be very difficult to land, suffered from power plant reliability issues, and were eclipsed in performance by contemporary jet fighters. The *Pogo* and *Salmon* became historical curiosities, regularly making the list of world's worst/strangest aircraft; the VTOL turboprop tailsitter configuration proved to be a dud.

This monograph focuses on the original compe-

1

tition which produced these ill-fated aircraft, specifically the proposal made by the Goodyear Aircraft Corporation of Akron, Ohio. Their proposal for the three-quarter scale demonstrator was designated as the GA-28A; the full scale fighter was designated GA-28B. Like Convair, Goodyear chose a delta wing layout for their VTOL fighter, though it differed considerably in other aspects, particularly in the landing gear.

The proposal documents for both the GA-28A and GA-28B were quite similar, with many sections being basically identical in content. For reasons of economy, I have combined them in the summary below, calling out key differences where necessary. The text is rather technical, as it was originally intended for BuAer engineers, but I decided to summarize the majority of it for those who appreciate such abstruse material. Accompanying the aircraft description are highly detailed schematics of both vehicles, which will likely be of interest to modelers and dedicated enthusiasts of aircraft design. While Goodyear was among the losers of the convoy fighter competition, serious engineering work went into their innovative and unorthodox proposal. The GA-28A/B really pushed the envelope of what was possible in 1950, showing that the company was definitely capable of designing more than blimps. While I don't think Goodyear would have fared any better than Convair or Lockheed in building and testing an actual aircraft, given the technological limitations of the day, I feel it is nonetheless important to preserve and disseminate a record of their proposal effort, however minor its place in aerospace history.

Features & Innovations

General Design Considerations. The Goodyear GA-28A was a three-quarter scale model prototype (proof of concept demonstrator) of the GA-28B convoy fighter, both of which were designed to fulfill the requirements laid out in OS-122. After careful consideration of the requirements and several different configurations, Goodyear determined that it was not only entirely feasible to eliminate auxiliary handling gear and incorporate the landing gear within the basic aircraft, but actually desirable to do so.

Before embarking on an all out effort for such an "ultimate airplane," a careful analysis was made of the dynamic landing loads involved in the vertical landing configuration from both the standpoint of alighting on its own gear and alighting on auxiliary gear. Surprisingly enough, the weight penalty required to handle the loads imposed on the airplane structure by merely setting the airplane on its tail

feathers, together with anticipated gust loads, was of such magnitude that carrying a completely adequate alighting gear at all times was reasonable. Further examination indicated that for very little additional weight penalty the airplane could be designed to land conventionally as well as vertically, giving the GA-28A/B a tremendous flexibility and safety above and beyond its initially conceived employment.

Ground Stability. Once this trend was definitely established, considerable time and effort was spent in endeavoring to arrive at a configuration which would provide satisfactory static stability on a pitching and rolling deck without auxiliary stabilizing means in order to eliminate all specialized handling gear. Obviously, this meant that some means had to be devised to lower the center of gravity of the airplane when it was in the vertical takeoff position. This resulted in shortening the airplane and eventually defined the GA-28A as a fundamentally tailless machine embodying 27.25° of static ground stability. That is, the deck would have to be inclined 27.25° before the stabilizing moment would reduce to zero. Since 20° of roll was generally believed to be the maximum likely to be encountered, the additional 7.25° provided a margin for inertia forces generated by deck roll in power off and landing conditions. The GA-28B was basically identical to the smaller airplane, except for having a static ground stability of 27.5°.

Takeoff presented a different and somewhat more complicated problem in that at high angles of deck roll, the upsetting thrust moment was of such magnitude as to overbalance the normal restoring moment. As a result, higher powers up to takeoff power could be applied and takeoff accomplished only within certain angular limits of deck roll, before overturning the airplane, unless means of restraint were employed.

General Purpose of Design. As the basic configuration progressed to the point where an operationally feasible airplane appeared possible, it occurred to Goodyear that the GA-28A, in addition to being useful as a research airplane, would be ideally suited for a transition training airplane. Therefore, this concept was pursued in the preparation of the design of the three-quarter scale model airplane.

General Appearance of Design. The artist's impressions depict the general appearance of the aircraft and define the basic configuration as a semi-delta, semi-midwing design with triple vertical tail surfaces and containing an alighting gear completely

adequate for either conventional or vertical landing and takeoff. The inclusion of a rotatable ejection seat, as suggested by a report from NADC Johnsville, was completely adequate and logical, but obviously

2) Artist's impression of the GA-28A in operation, showing its remarkable ability to take off and land both vertically and horizontally. Goodyear designed the type to be not only a research airplane, but a trainer as well.

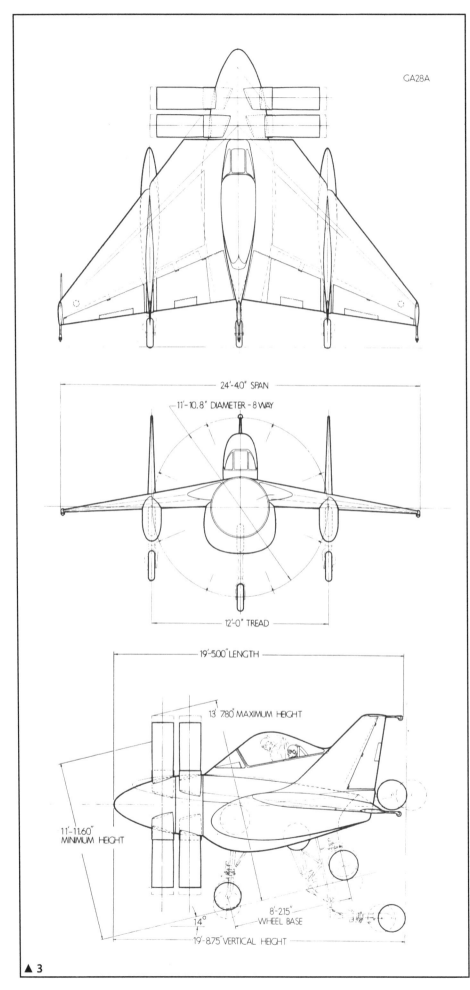

24'-4.0" SPAN

11'-10.8" DIAMETER - 8 WAY

12'-0" TREAD

19'-5.00" LENGTH

13'.780" MAXIMUM HEIGHT

11'-11.60" MINIMUM HEIGHT

14°

8'-2.15" WHEEL BASE

19'-8.75" VERTICAL HEIGHT

▲ 3

3) **Basic three-view of the Goodyear GA-28A showing landing gear positions for both horizontal and vertical attitudes.**

required a much larger cabin than was originally contemplated for the DR72 and DR72A airplanes. (These designations are referenced several times in the Goodyear proposal; they appear to have been earlier convoy fighter studies done by the Navy or Goodyear. Detailed information on them is presently lacking).

Seat Ejection. In keeping with the training airplane concept, clearance was provided in the GA-28A for ejecting the pilot with the seat in any position. For the GA-28B, clearance was provided for ejecting the pilot with the seat in the down position only. In the interest of space and weight saving, Goodyear noted that conventional and vertical adjustment of the seat was omitted and vertical adjustment was accomplished by rotating the seat up or down as desired.

General Data. The normal gross weight of the GA-28A transition training airplane with 45 minutes fuel aboard was 8,183 lbs; wing area 204 ft²; wing span 24.3 ft; overall height in vertical position 19 ft 8.75 in; overall height in conventional landing position 13 ft 7.8 in maximum and 11 ft 11.6 in minimum.

The normal gross weight of the GA-28B with 3,280 lbs fuel aboard was 16,994 lbs; wing area was 345 ft²; wing span 31.3 ft; overall height in vertical position 28.0625 ft; overall height in conventional landing position 14.8125 ft minimum and 16.9375 ft maximum. In the conventional attitude the dimensions were such that the GA-28B could be stowed in the hangar deck of a carrier.

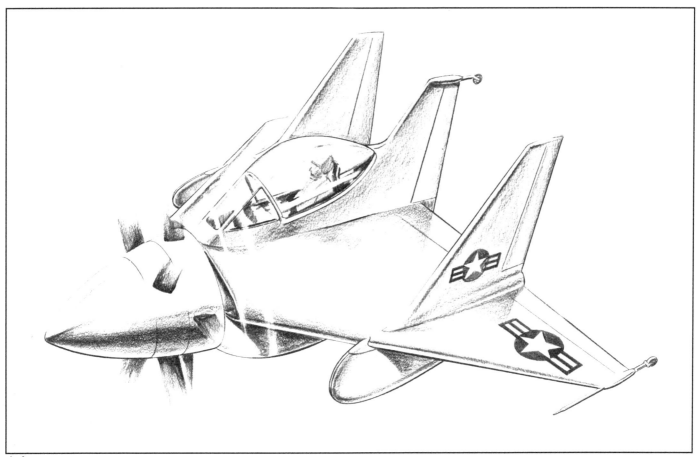

▲ 4

Ground Attitude. Goodyear felt that both the GA-28A and GA-28B should be self-contained airplanes completely capable of assuming either the conventional or vertical position on the ground without an external power source and able to land either conventionally or vertically by simply positioning the landing gear selector lever. A 3,000 PSI hydraulic system was provided as a source of power.

Single Engine Performance. Further, since the nature of the double Mamba engine made single engine operation possible, propeller feathering was provided for the GA-28A. The airplane could be trimmed to fly satisfactorily on a single engine, one propeller feathered, and landed in the conventional fashion. With both propellers feathered, the airplane would be fully controllable in a "Power Off" emergency conventional landing.

The GA-28B also featured propeller feathering and could be trimmed to fly on a single engine and land conventionally.

Producibility. To improve the producibility of both aircraft, Goodyear took some small weight penalties in their design. Examination of the inboard profile drawings shows that the aircraft were of conventional stringer and light skin construction

4) Artist's impression of the GA-28A prototype/trainer. Goodyear's interpretation of the OS-122 requirements resulted in a design which looked more like a caricature of an aircraft than an actual flying machine, but the company believed that it was the best solution to the specification.

with flush joints and riveting throughout. However, Goodyear noted that it was actively engaged in the production of a metal core sandwich material for industry-wide use and that as the actual design progressed, material weight saving could be realized by judicious use of sandwich construction. Further, provisions were made for feedershop installation of equipment in major structural subassemblies which would result in high production efficiency since the number of stations necessary on the final production line would be materially reduced.

Experimental Adjustments. Provisions were made on both aircraft to permit varying the dihedral angle by means of different length rigid links between the fuselage and the upper wing root attachment fitting.

Control System. The basic mixing of the elevon and aileron signals was accomplished by a bevel gear "mixer" unit to which the control stick was attached. Stability calculations indicated that it would be desirable to have the outboard elevons operate as elevons continually, whereas it was desirable for the inboard flaps to function as elevons only during vertical flight, and as ailerons only throughout the high speed and conventional landing conditions. To achieve this, a "sifter unit" was designed which enabled the pilot to select the control configuration desired. To reduce pilot burden, this selection was automatically made for the vertical landing gear configuration. However, the gear could be immediately retracted upon vertical take off without effecting the inboard elevon control, which could only be altered by direct selection of the pilot.

A one hundred percent boost artificial feel mass balanced elevon control system is shown in the inboard profiles. While Goodyear did not feel this system to be necessary on the small airplane, it was felt to be expedient to include it in order to achieve an indication of the suitability of this type of elevon control system for larger airplanes of this type under consideration. Only conventional mechanical linkage without boost was provided for the rudder controls of the GA-28A. The rudder controls of the GA-28B employed a "hydro power" proportional feel booster unit of 3.1 ratio.

Autopilot. To provide for automatic stabilization in cruising, transition and hovering flight, and to enable programming of take-

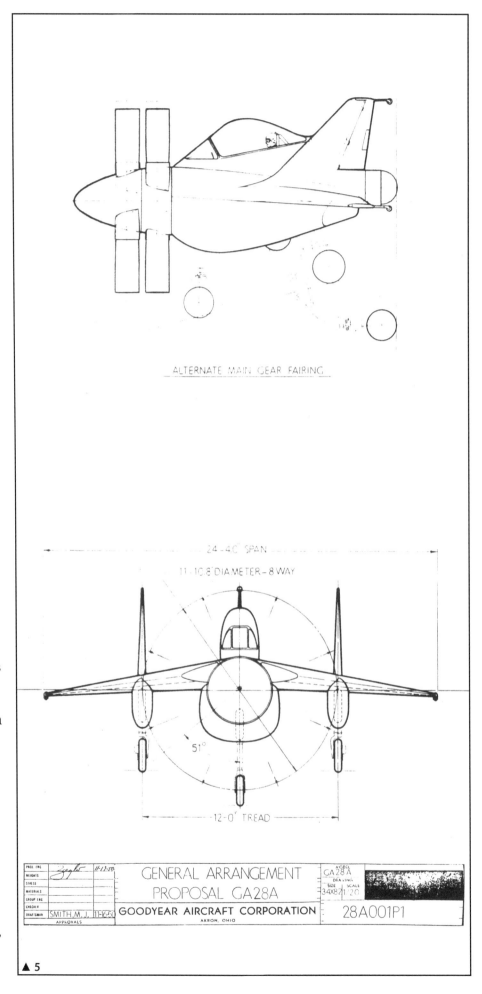

ALTERNATE MAIN GEAR FAIRING

24-4.0' SPAN

11-10.8 DIAMETER - 8 WAY

51°

12-0' TREAD

PROJ ENG	Ziegler	11-12-50	GENERAL ARRANGEMENT	A MODEL GA28A		
WEIGHTS				DRAWING		
STRESS			PROPOSAL GA28A	SIZE	SCALE	
MATERIALS				34X82	1/20	
GROUP ENG						
CHECKER			GOODYEAR AIRCRAFT CORPORATION	28A001P1		
DRAFTSMAN	SMITH, M. J.	11-30-50	AKRON, OHIO			
	APPROVALS					

▲ 5

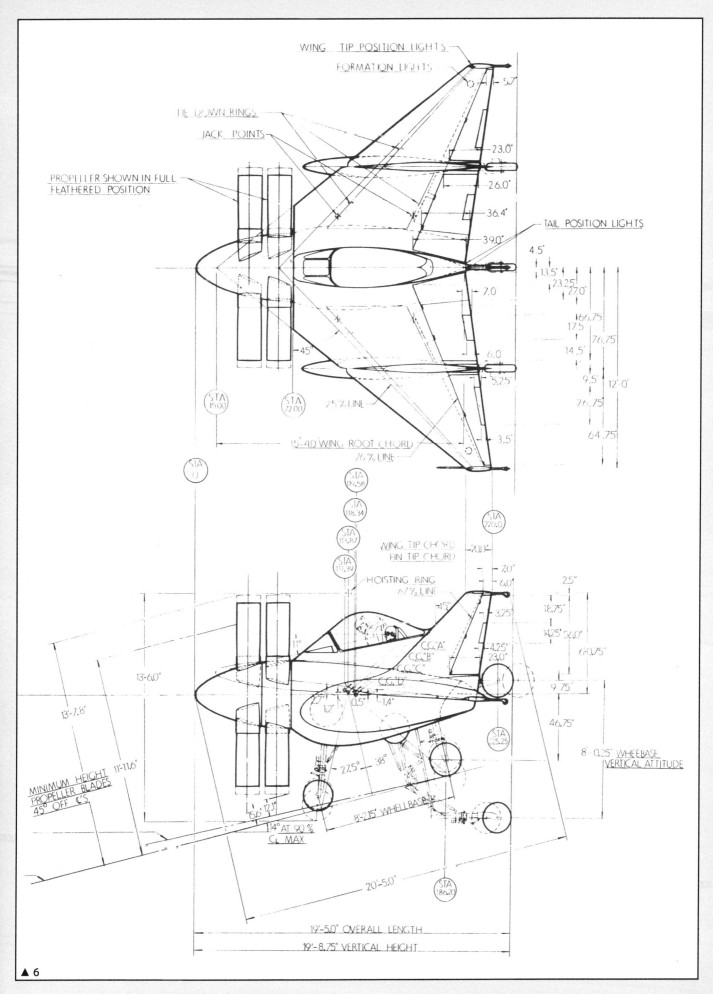

WING TIP POSITION LIGHTS
FORMATION LIGHTS

TIE DOWN RINGS
JACK POINTS

PROPELLER SHOWN IN FULL
FEATHERED POSITION

5.7°
23.0°
26.0°
36.4°
39.0°

TAIL POSITION LIGHTS

4.5°
13.5°
23.25°
27.0°

7.0°

66.75°
17.5°
76.75°
14.5°
9.5°
12'-0"
26.75°
64.75°

45°
6.0°
5.25°

STA
15.00

STA
72.00

25 % LINE

15'-4.0" WING ROOT CHORD
26 % LINE

3.5°

STA
0

STA
119.58

STA
118.34

STA
114.87

STA
111.39

WING TIP CHORD
FIN TIP CHORD

STA
220.0

20.0"

HOISTING RING
67 % LINE

7.0"
6.0"
2.5"

15°
3.25"

18.75"

C.G."A"
C.G."B"
C.G."C"
C.G."D"

4.25"
23.0°

14.25" 56.0"
6'-0.75"

11°

13'-6.0"

9.75"

13'-7.8"

1.2" 0.5" 1.4"

46.75"

8'-0.25" WHEEBASE
VERTICAL ATTITUDE

STA
225.25

11'-11.6"

MINIMUM HEIGHT
PROPELLER BLADES
45° OFF ⊄'S

5.6° 12.1°

27.5° 38°

8'-2.15" WHELLBASE

14° AT 90 %
CL MAX

STA
186.20

20'-5.0"

19'-5.0" OVERALL LENGTH
19'-8.75" VERTICAL HEIGHT

WING AREA (TOTAL) — .... ?84.?? SQ.FT.
  INBD. ELEVON (INCLUDING TABS & BAL. FWD. OF H.L.)
    UP ELEVON 30.30
    DOWN ELEVON 21.24
    TAB BALANCE 1.98
  OUTBD. ELEVON (INCLUDING TABS & BAL. FWD. OF H.L.) 15.80
    TABS-BALANCE & TRIM 1.62
VERTICAL TAIL AREA (TOTAL) 53.68
  OUTBOARD
    RUDDERS (INCLUDING TABS & BAL. FWD. OF H.L.) 13.56
    FINS (INCLUDING 1.60 SQ.FT. OF CONTAINED RUDDER BAL.) 29.80
    TABS-TRIM .... .73
    PADDLE BALANCE .... .22
  INBOARD
    RUDDER (INCLUDING BAL. FWD. OF H.L.) 6.81
    FIN (INCLUDING .63 SQ.FT. OF CONTAINED RUDDER BAL.) 5.52
CONTROL SURFACE ANGULAR TRAVEL
  INBOARD ELEVON .... ±37°
    ELEVATOR .... ±25°
    AILERON (CAN BE USED INDEPENDENTLY) .... ±12°
    TAB-BALANCE .... ±37°
  OUTBOARD ELEVON .... ±37°
    ELEVATOR .... ±25°
    AILERON .... ±12°
    TAB TRIM .... ±10°
    TAB-BALANCE .... ±37°
  RUDDERS .... ±25°
    TAB-TRIM .... ±13°
AIRFOIL SECTION
  WING NACA 65-A012
  VERTICAL TAIL 65-A009
WING INCIDENCE .... +2°
WING DIHEDRAL .... -5°
MEAN AERODYNAMIC CHORD — .... 124.00"
  TO L.E.MAC. FROM FUSELAGE STATION 0 .... 82.50"
  TO L.E.MAC. FROM THRUST LINE .... 9.00"
  TO L.E.MAC. FROM C.L. AIRPLANE .... 52.30"
LANDING GEAR TIRES
  MAIN GEAR (2)
    TYPE PD 476 MIL C 5041
    SIZE 24X5.5
    PLY 14
  NOSE GEAR (1)
    TYPE PD 474 MIL C 5041
    SIZE 22X5.5
    PLY 10
WING ANGLE OF ATTACK CORRESPONDING TO THE FOLLOWING
VALUES OF C_L (MAX):

% C_L (MAX)	ANGLE OF ATTACK
90%	16°
75%	12.5°
50%	8.2°
110% Vs POWER OFF	15.0°

C.G. "A" BASIC CONFIGURATION
C.G. "B" NORMAL LANDING CONFIGURATION
C.G. "C" VERTICAL TAKE-OFF CONFIGURATION
C.G. "D" VERTICAL LANDING LESS 90% FUEL CONFIGURATION

▲ 7 ▼ 8

COCKPIT PLAN

L.H. CONSOLE   INSTRU. PANEL   R.H. CONSOLE

7) A comprehensive table of the GA-28A's major characteristics taken from the blueprint shown in the previous spread.

8) A detailed plan of the cockpit layout taken from the inboard profile blueprint.

9) Inboard profile of the GA-28A showing the location of major equipment and structural members.

off to cruise and cruise to landing flight paths, an automatic pilot was installed in both aircraft. This unit was basically a modification of the Sperry X-4 autopilot, with three integrating rate gyros and an accelerometer which served as sensing elements of yaw, pitch, roll, and thrust line velocity motions of the airplane respectively. These indications were fed into amplifiers and thence were transmitted into airplane movement through the control system power units, and the engine power-control linkages. Manual stick override was achieved by a simple button engage switch on the pilot control stick, while throttle override was direct, manually imposed motion of the throttle overcoming the small inertia of the light power control servo during all non-automatic operation.

The pilot could utilize the autopilot in one of four possible modes. Selection was accomplished by a Command Selector knob on the instrument panel with dial positions for:

1) Autopilot control of the plane in cruising or hovering flight;

2) Pilot control of the airplane in any flight configuration through the autopilot via a "formation stick";

3) Automatic control sequencing for cruise to hovering transition;

4) Automatic control sequencing for hovering or takeoff to cruise transition; and

5) Autopilot "off"—the formation stick control was the conventional miniature control stick conveniently located forward and to the right of the right arm rest, and was operated in the same manner as the standard control

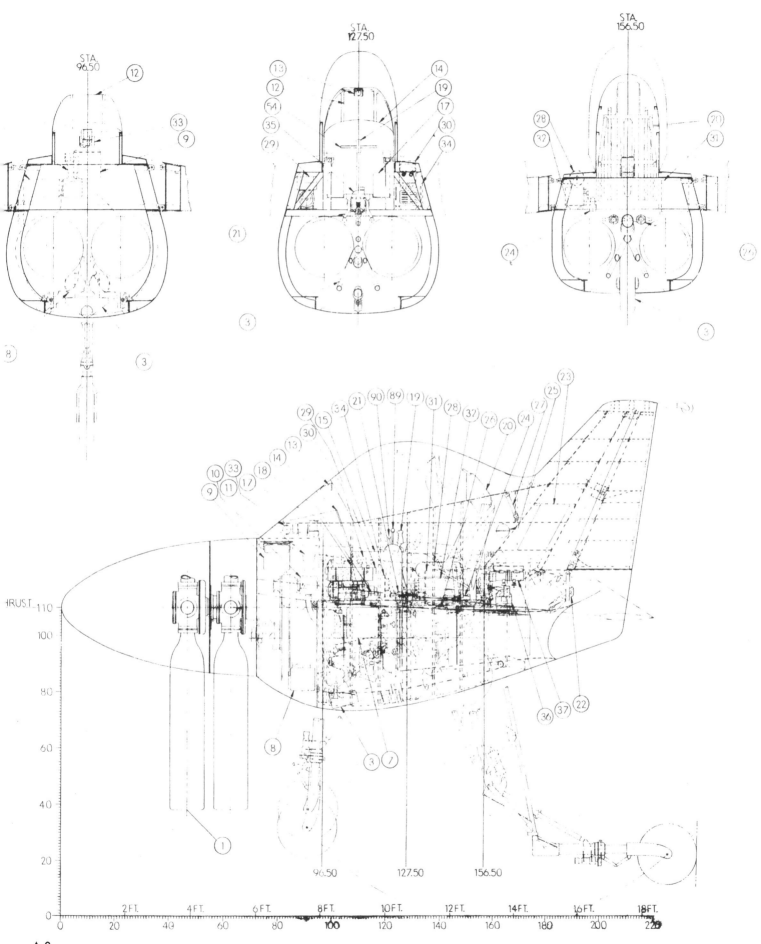

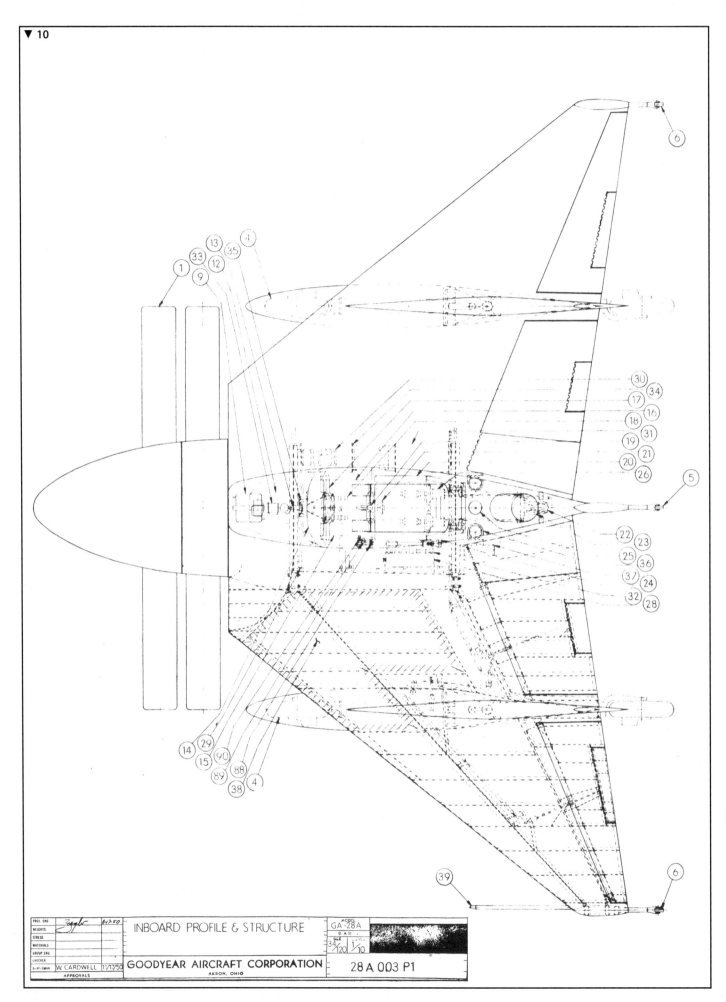

INBOARD PROFILE & STRUCTURE

GOODYEAR AIRCRAFT CORPORATION
AKRON, OHIO

PROJ. ENG	Ziegler	11-2-50
WEIGHTS		
STRESS		
MATERIALS		
GROUP ENG		
CHECKER		
DRAFTSMAN	W. CARDWELL	11/17/50
APPROVALS		

MODEL GA-28A

28 A 003 P1

10) Top inboard profile of the Goodyear GA-28A.

11) Legend for the inboard profile blueprint reproduced on pp. 8-10.

---

stick to give pitch and roll, and to give yaw via a small heading knob at the top of the pistol grip shaped arm.

It was entirely feasible to also include two additional automatic control features. One was the "load-limit computer" or regulator to prevent inadvertent overstressing during maneuvers. This instrument would operate as a "g" restrictor for the airplane, using accelerometers as sensing means. The other device, governed by solenoid action and monitored by the airspeed indicator, would control the operation of the "sifter" mechanism.

Quick Power Plant Change Unit. The power plant proposal drawings for both aircraft depict a power plant quick-change unit and transporting dolly that would permit a complete power plant change to be accomplished in 30 minutes or less. If the self-contained unit had been previously checked out by running on a test stand or another airplane, no additional time would be required to adjust the power plant controls.

To accomplish a power plant change for the GA-28A, the lower forward plenum chamber cowl and the lower rear fuselage panels were removed, standard Navy jacks placed under the front beam jack pads and the nose gear extended in the knuckled position by means of closing certain hydraulic valves and using the hydraulic hand pump. This permitted a crossbar to be inserted between the two rear engine hoist points. Three men then positioned the three-legged dolly under the engine; one man adjusted the ex-

1 PROPELLERS(2)	61 FUEL PRESS.(DUAL)
2 POWER PLANT -DOUBLE MAMBA	62 HYDRAULIC PRESS.
3 NOSE GEAR	63 OIL PRESS (DUAL)
4 MAIN LANDING GEAR(2)	64 REAR BEARING TEMP. (DUAL)
5 FIN TIP BUMPER	65 AMMETER - VOLTMETER
6 WING TIP BUMPERS(2)	66 INVERTER SWITCH
7 OIL TANKS(2)	67 WARNING LIGHT
8 OIL COOLERS(2)	68 SECONDARY BUSS SWITCH
9 BATTERY	69 BATTERY- GENERATOR SWITCH
10 GENERATOR	70 WARNING LIGHT
11 HYDRAULIC PUMP	71 CO_2 AGENT SWITCH
12 BULLET PROOF WINDSHIELD	72 FIRE WARNING LIGHT
13 STANDBY COMPASS	73 PITOT HEAT SWITCH
14 INSTRUMENT PANEL	74 ALTERNATE STATIC PRESS. SWITCH
15 L.H. CONSOLE	75 LANDING GEAR POSIT. INDICATOR
16 R.H. CONSOLE	76 WARNING LIGHT
17 RUDDER PEDALS	77 MAIN GEAR CASTERING LOCK
18 BRAKE CYL.(2)	78 LANDING GEAR CONTROL- 3 POSIT.
19 CONTROL STICK	79 ELEVON CONTROL
20 PILOT EJECTION SEAT	L.H. CONSOLE
21 MIXER	80 OXYGEN REGULATOR
22 SIFTER	81 OIL DILUTION SWITCH
23 HYDRAULIC RESERVOIR	82 FUEL CROSS-OVER SWITCH
24 HAND PUMP	83 TRIM TAB CONTROL
25 ACCUMULATOR	84 ENGINE FUEL SHUT-OFF SWITCHES(2)
26 ELEVON BOOSTER CYL.(2)	85 PRIMER SWITCHES(2)
27 CANOPY ACCUATOR CYL.	86 FUEL BOOSTER PUMP SWITCHES(2)
28 OXYGEN BOTTLE	87 TANK SHUT-OFF SWITCHES(2)
29 A.C. INVERTER	88 SEAT POSIT. SWITCH
30 A.C. VOLTAGE REG.	89 ENGINE POWER CONTROLS(2)
31 ARC-27 TRANS-RECEIVER	90 PROPELLER FEATHERING CONTROLS(2)
32 APN-1 TRANS-RECEIVER	91 MASTER IGNITION SWITCHES(2)
33 E-4 AUTO PILOT GYROS(3)	R.H. CONSOLE
34 AMP.	92 ARC-27 CONTROL
35 RUDDER SERVO	93 PRE-EJECTION LEVER
36 ELEVON SERVOS(2)	94 AUTO PILOT MAGNITUDE CONTROL
37 SERVO CONTROL	95 SWITCH
38 FUEL TANK(L.H. & R.H.)	96 B-3 FLIGHT CONTROL
39 PITOT TUBE	97 CIRCUIT BREAKER PANEL
PILOTS INSTRU. PANEL	
40 FREE AIR TEMP.	
41 ACCELEROMETER - AUTO PILOT	
42 CLOCK	
43 APN-1 ALTIMETER	
44 AIRSPEED INDICATOR	
45 GYRO HORIZAN	
46 RATE OF CLIMB	
47 TACHOMETER (DUAL)	
48 TORQUEMETER (DUAL)	
49 TURN & BANK	
50 DIRECTIONAL GYRO	
51 SENSITIVE ALTIMETER	
52 APN-1 ALT. LIMIT SWITCH	
53 WARNING LIGHT	
54 CHART BOARD	
55 FUEL FLOWMETER (DUAL)	
56 FUEL QUANTITY GAGE -LEFT TANK	
57 -RIGHT TANK	
58 OIL TEMP.(DUAL)	
59 TURBINE TEMP. (DUAL)	
60 TRIM TAB INDICATOR	

▲ 11

tendable engine nose case support by means of a hydraulic hand pump located on the rear vertical leg and each of the other men simply adjusted one of the two vertical leg extensions until they engaged and the crossbar attached to the two engine (rear) hoist points. To complete the removal of the quick change unit, it was only necessary to remove the safetying and rotate three small levers. One of these levers was

12) Artist's impression of the full scale Goodyear GA-28B convoy fighter taking off from the forward deck of a merchant vessel. Such ships would have required relatively minor modifications to operate the aircraft, as Goodyear's design featured retractable landing gear and a minimum of auxiliary handling and recovery equipment.

located at each of the three engine mount fittings. The unit was then free to be towed away with the first inch of forward travel disconnecting all fluid and electrical connections.

The replacement unit, installed on another dolly, was simply pushed into the proper position, adjusted to the proper height by means of the three hand hydraulic pumps and the tapered male engine attachment fittings pushed into the tapered female engine mount fitting which aligned and connected all fluid and electrical connections. The installation was secured by rotating and safetying the three engine mount levers. The lower plenum chamber cowling was replaced and the power plant unit was completely installed since all power plant controls operated through common center balance plates, one attached to the basic airplane structure and one attached to the engine, with movement of the controls being accomplished by wobbling of the plate with no through attachment being involved. It was only necessary to retract the nose gear by means of the hydraulic hand pump and the airplane was ready to fly. In addition to access to the engine compartment via the landing gear wells and by removal of the lower forward plenum chamber and lower rear fuselage cowls, other necessary small inspection doors were provided.

The power plant change for the GA-28B was very similar, except for some minor details unique to the construction of the larger aircraft.

Cockpit Access and Egress. With the airplane in the vertical attitude on the ground, access to and egress from the cockpit was easily achieved by flush type hand and toe holds located in the cabin side and top surface of the wing root skin. When the airplane was in the conventional attitude on the ground, access was by means of a small ladder over the leading edge of the wing and thence by conventional flush type hand holds to the cockpit. Since space was not available to open the canopy by sliding it aft in the conventional manner, it was hinged at the trailing edge and the front was elevated for entrance. Cabin jettisoning was provided.

Landing Gear. Free swiveling of both the main and nose gear was provided in either the conventional or vertical landing configuration. Appropriate self-centering shimmy dampeners were provided on each of the gears as well as a selector lock so that if desired, the main wheels could be prevented from swiveling. When the GA-28A was to be landed cross wind conventionally, it was probably desirable to land the airplane with all three wheels unlocked in order to avoid the generation of marginal overturn-

ing moments. Ground stability of the GA-28B in the conventional landing configuration was normal, and the airplane would, in most cases, be landed with the main gear locked. It was obviously mandatory that both airplanes be landed in the vertical configuration with all wheels free to swivel. Centering devices were provided on all wheels so that the direction of rotation was parallel to the ship's center line for retraction.

Goodyear noted that with the unusual disposition of weight, that is more weight on the nose wheel in the conventional landing attitude than on the main wheels, the brakes were not quite as effective as might normally be expected. However, including the desirable low speed drag effects of the contra-rotating dual propeller, the GA-28A could be stopped in 22.3 seconds with a landing roll of 1,850 ft. The GA-28B could be stopped in 21 seconds with a landing roll of 1,950 ft. Reversible propellers were provided for the larger aircraft which enabled it to stop in 500 ft.

The landing gear was designed to fall free and lock down unassisted in the conventional landing gear position, but a hydraulic hand pump was provided as an additional safety measure.

Brake System. Power boosted "hydro power" brake cylinders installed horizontally on the rudder pedal paralleling arms were provided. These were dual purpose cylinders and when manually boosted by the airplane's hydraulic system, provided a powerful, nice-feeling brake at normal pedal loads but contained the added safety feature of functioning as a straight master cylinder in the event of hydraulic power failure.

Fuel Tanks. Goodyear proposed integral wing fuel tanks in the interest of simplification, space and weight saving. These were chosen because self-sealing tanks were not required; a relatively smooth propeller turbine power plant was installed on a very rigid wing structure; the combination of features peculiar to this configuration—vertical dive, vertical hovering, transition to horizontal flight; and the reevaluation of progress made in the development of rubber based aromatic fuel proof sealing compounds. For the GA-28B, bladder type seals would have been installed in the two fuselage tanks as an additional safety feature since leakage of fuel in this area might find its way into the engine compartment immediately underneath the cockpit floor.

Deck Protection. In view of close proximity of the jet exhausts to the deck in the vertical takeoff

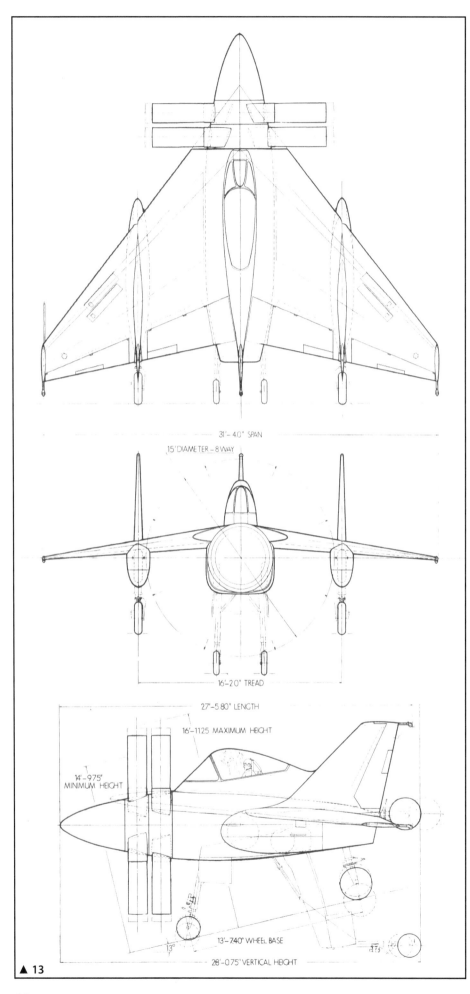

13) Basic three-view of the Good-year GA-28B convoy fighter showing landing gear positions for both horizontal and vertical attitudes; note the dual wheel nose gear.

31'–4.0" SPAN

15' DIAMETER – 8 WAY

16'–2.0" TREAD

27'–5.80" LENGTH

16'–11.25 MAXIMUM HEIGHT

14'–9.75' MINIMUM HEIGHT

13'–7.40" WHEEL BASE

13°

28'–0.75" VERTICAL HEIGHT

▲ 13

and landing configuration, it was pointed out that it would probably be necessary to have the deck protected from the local concentration of heat.

Tire Protection. Since the deck would serve to deflect the heat sidewise across the deck, it might have been necessary to provide small vertical heat shields for the main and nose gear tires as special equipment.

Goodyear also prepared an alternate main wheel landing gear fairing for the GA-28A. If the close proximity of the nose of the existing landing gear fairing proved troublesome from a propeller vibration point of view, resort to this type of fairing (approximately equivalent drag characteristics) was contemplated.

Landing Load Analysis. With the concept of the self-contained landing gear as being both feasible and highly practicable, the consideration of geometry and structural mounting became the paramount study. From the former standpoint, it was necessary to locate the wheels in conventional and tail first landing attitudes so as to achieve both stability in landing and in secured on-deck service conditions, as well as to restrict imposed landing loads to reasonable values. A byproduct of the short wheel base was the unconventional location of the center of gravity closer to the nose wheel than to the main gear. This caused high loads at the nose gear. The latter condition defined the critical loads for the forward gear, and was analyzed in the same fashion as a bicycle arrangement.

In the tail first attitude, the airplane had to be capable of alighting on a rolling and pitching deck with extreme inclinations of 20° and 5° respectively, as well as maintaining position with a 15 knot ship way in a 20 knot wind from any quarter; heave of the ship was neglected.

Once the aircraft touched the deck with any extremity, it was effectively uncontrollable, with two extreme landing conditions being evident. The first considered forward inclination of the airplane thrust axis of 13.5° for hovering into a 35 knot relative wind. This angle was additive to a bow-down ship pitch of 5° for initial contact of the nose gear with subsequent rotation of the airplane to contact of the main gear. For the existing configuration, this mode was not critical. The second, cartwheeling into a 20° rolled deck in the wing plane, yielded high design loads. In this mode the airplane, inclined in yaw 7.5° against a 20 knot wind, struck first on the wing tip, necessitating the wing tip bumper wheel and shock strut, rotating down onto one main gear, and thence continued rotation to the other main gear. Goodyear noted that the 20° roll condition was considered extreme, and therefore, all loads calculated on the basis of that angle would be conservative.

Design loads were determined using landing de-

14) Exploded view of the GA-28B showing the major components of this bizarre and interesting design. Note the eight-blade contra-rotating propeller, which set it apart from the Convair XFY-1 and Lockheed XFV-1, both equipped with six-blade units.

sign gross weight (i.e. takeoff gross weight minus 60 percent fuel) at 10 ft per second sinking speed. Loads were also calculated for takeoff design gross weight at 10 ft/second sinking speed, and for both landing and takeoff weights at 17 ft/second, and the effects on the airplane for each of the latter three conditions established.

Armament Installation (GA-28B). Once the configuration had progressed to the point that it was obvious that external landing gear fairings were mandatory, it became possible to make practically an ideal armament installation. Two 20 mm guns were installed on the insides immediately under the wing and totally enclosed in the landing gear fairing. By locating the guns on their sides with the cradles facing each other immediately under the heavy landing gear rib structure, it was possible to provide a simple lightweight trunion mounting easily accessible through the landing gear doors

PROJ ENG		
WEIGHTS		
STRESS		
MATERIALS		
GROUP ENG		
CHECKER		
DRAFTSMAN		
APPROVALS		

GENERAL ARRANGEMENT
PROPOSAL GA28B
GOODYEAR AIRCRAFT CORPORATION
AKRON, OHIO

MODEL
GA 28B
SIZE | SCALE
1/24

28001P1

15) A more detailed general arrangement of the GA-28B with additional measurements and other information added. Note the small three-view to the immediate lower right showing an alternate version with the wing pods deleted and inward folding main gear; this modification was estimated to increase the maximum speed by 25 kts and enabled an increase in propeller diameter, improving its efficiency.

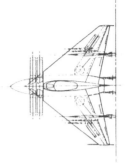

PROP
FEATH

ALTERNATE MAIN GEAR RETRACTION
(SHOWING LANDING GEAR FAIRING ELIMINATED)

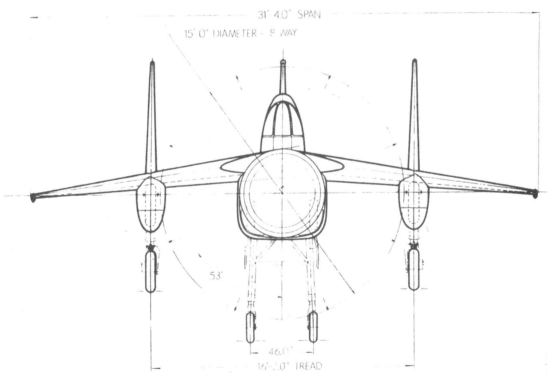

31' 4.0" SPAN

15' 0" DIAMETER – 8 WAY

THRUST LINE

5.3'

46.0"

16'-2.0" TREAD

GROUND LINE – MAIN
DEFLECTED, NOSE GEAR
COMPRESSED, & TIRE F

GROUND LINE – MAIN
TIRES & SHOCKS STA
DEFLECTED

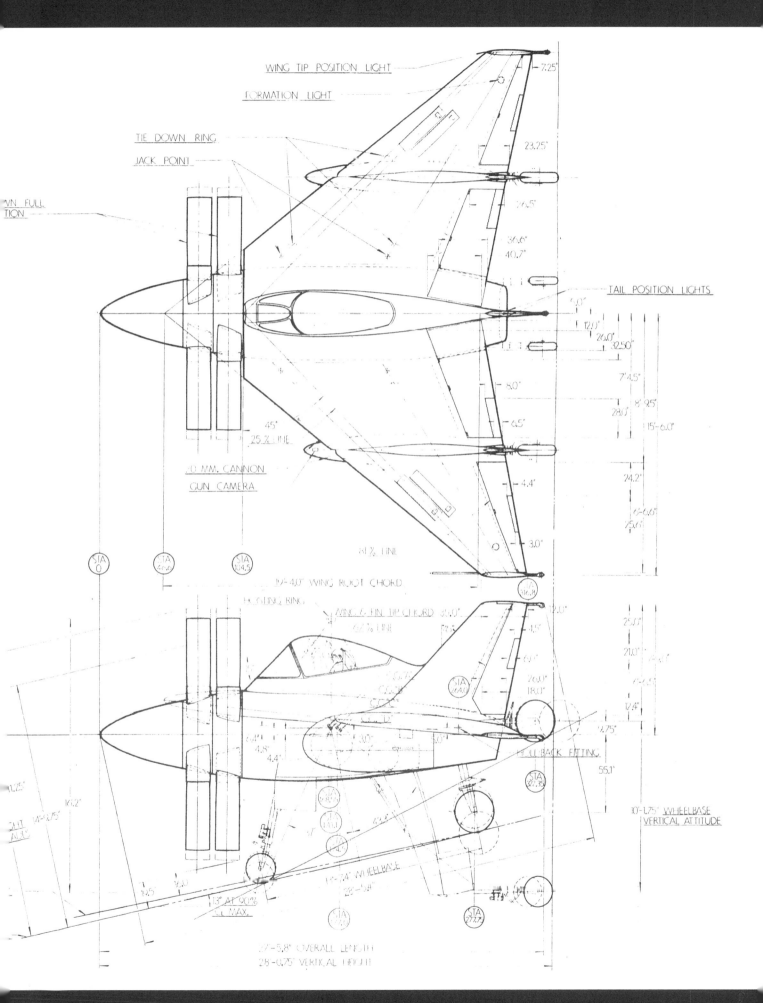

WING TIP POSITION LIGHT

FORMATION LIGHT

TIE DOWN RING

JACK POINT

WN FULL
TION

TAIL POSITION LIGHTS

7.25"

23.25"

26.5"

36.6"
40.7"

5.0"

12.0"
26.0"
32.50"

7'-4.5"

8'-9.5"

28.0"

15'-6.0"

24.2"

6'-6.0"
25.6"

45°
25 % LINE

40 MM. CANNON
GUN CAMERA

8.0"

6.5"

4.4"

3.0"

81 % LINE

STA
0

STA
40.6

STA
104.5

19'-4.0" WING ROOT CHORD

HOISTING RING

WING & FIN TIP CHORD 35.0"

62 % LINE

12.0"

4.5"

6.0"

26.0"
18.0"

STA
244.0

25.0"

21.0"

12.4"

2.75"

55.1"

STA
207.75

PULLBACK FITTING

10'-1.75" WHEELBASE
VERTICAL ATTITUDE

16.2"

14'-2.75"

1.25"

GHT
ALDG

14'-7.4" WHEELBASE
22'-5/4"

13° AT 90%
CL MAX.

STA
277.75

37'-5.8" OVERALL LENGTH
28'-0.75" VERTICAL HEIGHT

WING AREA (TOTAL)	345.0 SQ.FT.
INBD. ELEVON (INCLUDING TABS & BAL. FWD. OF HL)	
UP ELEVONS	42.42
DOWN ELEVONS	30.66
TAB-BALANCE	2.82
OUTBD. ELEVONS (INCLUDING TABS & BAL. FWD. OF HL)	18.98
TABS-BALANCE & TRIM	1.82
VERTICAL TAIL AREA (TOTAL)	97.91
OUTBOARD	
RUDDERS (INCLUDING TABS & BAL. FWD. OF HL)	25.83
FINS (INCLUDING 2.81 SQ. FT. OF CONTAINED RUDDER BAL.)	52.41
TABS-TRIM	1.53
PADDLE BALANCE	.31
INBOARD	
RUDDER INCLUDING TABS & BAL. FWD. OF HL)	12.65
FIN (INCLUDING 1.43 SQ. FT. OF CONTAINED RUDDER BAL.)	14.89 SQ.FT.
CONTROL SURFACE ANGULAR TRAVEL	
INBOARD ELEVON	±37°
ELEVATOR	±25°
AILERON (CAN BE USED INDEPENDENTLY)	±12
TAB BALANCE	±37°
OUTBOARD ELEVON	±37°
ELEVATOR	±25°
AILERON	±12°
TAB-TRIM	±10°
TAB BALANCE	±37°
RUDDERS	±25°
TAB-TRIM	±10°
AIRFOIL SECTION	
WING-NACA 65.A009	
VERTICAL TAIL NACA 65.A009	
WING INCIDENCE	2°
WING DIHEDRAL	5°
MEAN AERODYNAMIC CHORD	157.73
TO L.E.MAC. FROM FUSELAGE STATION 0	135.5
TO L.E.MAC. FROM THRUST LINE	15.3°
TO L.E.MAC. FROM CL AIRPLANE	0.0
LANDING GEAR TIRES	
MAIN GEAR (2)	
TYPE PD 497 MIL. S013A	
SIZE 30X7.7	
PLY 16	
NOSE GEAR (2)	
TYPE PD474 MILC S041	
SIZE 22X5.5	
PLY 10	
WING ANGLE OF ATTACK CORRESPONDING TO THE FOLLOWING VALUES OF CL(MAX)	

% CL(MAX)	ANGLE OF ATTACK
90%	15°
75%	12°
50%	8°
110% VS POWER OFF	15°

C.G. "A" BASIC CONFIGURATION	
C.G. "B" NORMAL LANDING CONFIGURATION	
C.G. "C" VERTICAL TAKE-OFF CONFIGURATION	
C.G. "D" VERTICAL LANDING LESS 90% FUEL CONFIGURATION	

▲ 16

for installing, removing and boresighting the guns which together with the quick-opening small doors over the feed mechanism made possible easy arming of the weapon on the deck when under blacked-out conditions. Built-in wing ammunition storage boxes (150 rounds per gun) were provided in the interest of weight saving (approximately 10 lbs per gun), easily accessible from the top side of the wing through a quick-opening door mechanism. Goodyear emphasized the compactness and straight-forwardness of this installation.

Armor plate in the form of bullet-proof glass was provided ahead of the pilot and conventional armor placed immediately abaft of the seat. No floor armor was provided since it was felt that the installation

of the power plant immediately below the cockpit floor provided adequate protection from below.

Further inspection of the armament drawing shows that installation of the MK6, Model 2 sight was not feasible and installation of an alternate sight should be considered.

Further Configuration Possibilities (GA-28B). Goodyear felt the performance figures contained in the performance summary of their report to be conservative. A careful review of the proposal suggested that a possible future configuration of improved vertical flight characteristics and capable of considerably higher speed could be achieved by a twin engine configuration embracing outboard located engines installed in an enlarged landing gear nacelle, single rotation supersonic propellers and a smaller, more conventionally shaped fuselage.

Alternate Landing Gear/ Armament Installation (GA-28B). When it became apparent that the addition of the simple external landing gear fairing, also originally thought desirable from the armament installation point of view, was prohibitive from high speed considerations (-25 kts), Goodyear designed an alternate landing gear installation, retracting the wheels completely within the wing. This improved the overall appearance and performance.

Time constraints prevented Goodyear from showing the alternate 20 mm cannon installation in their armament proposal drawing. However, a preliminary layout showed that the two cannons could be installed within the wing outboard of the landing gear position in a smoothly faired installation similar to the fairing shown on the DR72 airplane.

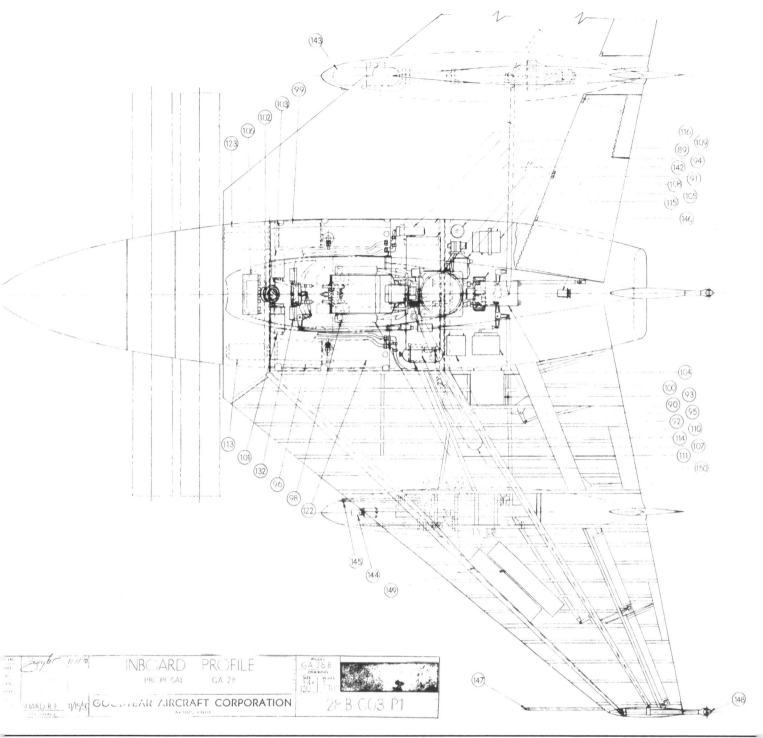

▲ 17

Hydraulic System

General. The main hydraulic system was a 3,000 PSI system and operated the landing gear, surface controls, sifter actuator and power boosted brakes. The landing gear section of the system was automatically depressurized in flight. Ground test connections were provided for maintenance purposes. A hand pump was installed for emergency operation. The fluid used was non-flammable in accordance with the BuAer specification.

In the original report, Goodyear went into great detail regarding the pumping system, surface control hydraulic system, and landing gear hydraulic system;

17) Inboard top view of the Goodyear GA-28B showing the disposition of major equipment and structural members.

this is omitted here due to the highly technical nature of the material, which is of minimal interest to the typical enthusiast.

Gear Retraction Time (GA 28B). The time required to fully retract the handling gear from the vertical takeoff position was estimated to be 11 to 14.95 seconds depending on the requirements of the boost system. This time was a result of the large fluid volumes and consequently large cylinders required

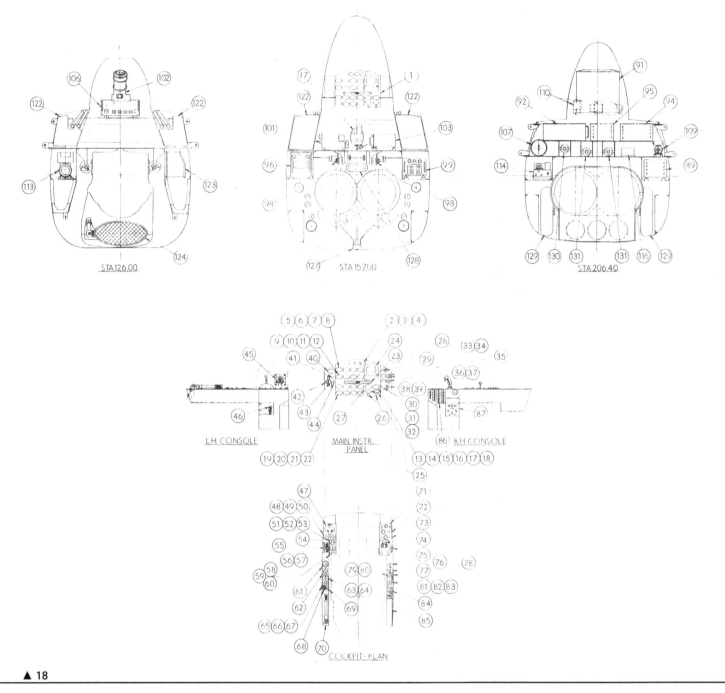

STA 126.00

STA 157.00

STA 206.40

LH CONSOLE

MAIN INSTR. PANEL

R.H. CONSOLE

COCKPIT-PLAN

to place the airplane in the vertical position without auxiliary power. However, if this retraction time was found to penalize unduly the time required to effect transition, the addition of two extra pumps would enable the gear to be retracted in 4.65 seconds.

Performance Summary

The GA-28A airplane was basically a ¾ scale version of the GA-28B convoy fighter design. Both versions were powered by turboprop engines driving dual-rotation propellers. The GA-28A was designed to be the prototype model which would furnish performance comparable to the GA-28B in vertical, hovering and transition phases of flight.

A unique design feature of the GA-28A/B was the ability to perform conventional-type landings and takeoffs, in addition to the specified vertical landing and takeoff.

Only moderate level-flight performance was obtained, mainly because there was no gearshift in the prototype specified engine-propeller combination. Maximum vertical acceleration, on the order of 8 ft/second, could be expected from the prototype airplane. Transitions from vertical to horizontal flight, and the reverse, could be made smoothly without abrupt maneuvers. Maximum rate of climb at sea level was 6,250 fpm. Service ceiling was 29,300 ft, while time to climb to 20,000 ft on military power was 6.2 minutes. Maximum level flight velocity was 320 knots at sea level and 315 knots at 20,000 ft altitude.

The GA-28B airplane was a tailless type aircraft incorporating a modified triangular wing planform which utilized NACA low-drag airfoil sections. The

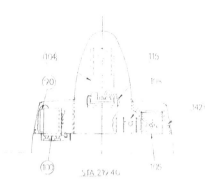

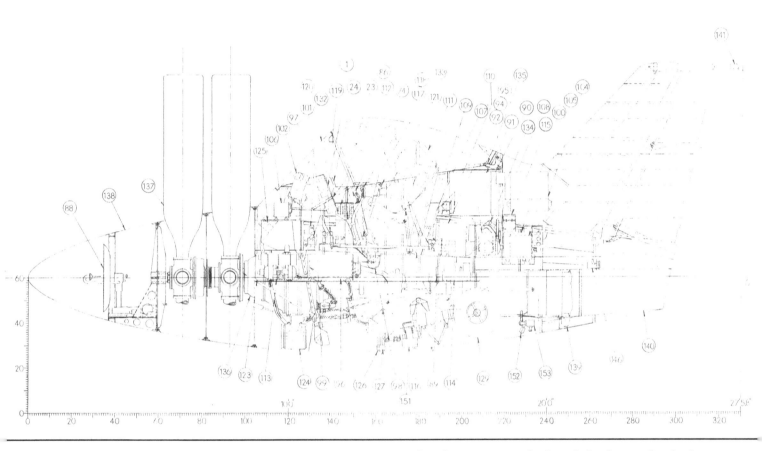

18) Side inboard profile, fuselage cross sections, and cockpit layout of the GA-28B convoy fighter; note the tilting seat to enable the pilot to land the aircraft in the vertical position, which proved to be no easy feat with either the Convair or Lockheed vehicles.

airplane was designed to meet the basic requirements of vertical takeoff from the deck of a ship, ability to hover in a vertical position and ability to make smooth transition into conventional level flight. In addition, it presented the high all-around performance required of a fighter type aircraft. An additional feature was its ability to take off or land in a conventional manner with its specially designed landing gear. Initial transition could be accomplished as a gradual pushover with a minimum acceleration along the flight path of approximately 8 ft/sec², and could be accomplished from zero velocity on a carrier deck to 150 knots level flight at 1,000 ft of altitude. Final transition from level flight to vertical landing was accomplished as a gradual slowing of airplane velocity as the attitude angle was increased, along with variation in engine throttle settings, until an

attitude of 90° was reached and the forward velocity was zero. This transition could be made with a minimum total change in altitude consistent with OS-122. A conventional takeoff could be accomplished in zero wind with a ground run of 1,035 ft. A 30 knot headwind reduced this distance to only 640 ft. This indicated the possibility of conventional landings and takeoffs from aircraft carriers.

Maximum rate of climb at sea level on military power was 10,000 ft/min. Time to climb from standstill to 35,000 ft with vertical takeoff was approximately 5.7 minutes. Attainment of combat radius under specified conditions permitted 1 hour 20 minute time for loiter at 35,000 ft before mission was started. Maximum velocity was 500 knots and minimum radius of turn was 18,700 ft at 420 knots.

The improvement in performance resulting from

1 MAIN INSTRUMENT PANEL

2 FREE AIR TEMPERATURE
3 ACCELEROMETER - AUTO PILOT
4 CLOCK
5 TACHOMETER (DUAL)
6 RATE OF CLIMB
7 GYRO - HORIZONTAL
8 AIR SPEED & MACH METER
9 TORQUE METER
10 TURN & BANK
11 DIRECTIONAL GYRO
12 ALTIMETER
13 TURBINE TEMPERATURE (DUAL)
14 OIL TEMPERATURE
15 COCKPIT ALTIMETER
16 RADIO ALTIMETER
17 FUEL PRESSURE
18 FUEL FLOW (DUAL)
19 REAR BEARING TEMPERATURE (DUAL)
20 OIL PRESSURE
21 HYDRAULIC PRESSURE
22 RADIO ALTIMETER SELECTOR
23 CHART BOARD
24 INDICATOR - AN/APS-25
25 FUEL QUANTITY (2)
26 WARNING LIGHT - 30 MIN. FUEL REMAINING
27 RADIO ALTIMETER WARNING LIGHT
28 FIRE WARNING LIGHT
29 CO_2 AGENT SWITCH
30 BATTERY VOLT-AMPMETER
31 AC VOLTMETER
32 AC VOLTMETER PHASE SELECTOR
33 WARNING LIGHT GEN. OFF
34 WARNING LIGHT ALT. OFF
35 GENERATOR ON SWITCH
36 SECONDARY BUSS SWITCH
37 ALTERNATOR SWITCH
38 INVERTER SWITCH
39 WARNING LIGHT - INVERTER OFF
40 LANDING GEAR & ELEVON POSITION IND.
41 WARNING LIGHT - LANDING GEAR UNLOCKED
42 MAIN WHEEL CASTERING LOCK
43 LANDING GEAR CONTROL - 3 POSITION
44 ELEVON CONTROL HANDLE

LEFT HAND CONSOLE

45 CHART - FUEL SYSTEM DIAGRAM
46 RADAR SCANNER CONTROL - AN/APS-25
47 OXYGEN REG. VALVE
48 BOOSTER PUMP SWITCH (L & R)
49 FUEL TANK SHUT-OFF SWITCH (L & R)
50 FUEL CROSS-FEED SWITCH
51 FUEL SHUT-OFF SWITCH (LEFT ENG. SECTION)
52 FUEL SHUT-OFF SWITCH (RIGHT ENG. SECTION)
53 FUEL BALANCE SWITCH
54 PROPELLER FEATHERING CONTROL
55 POWER LEVER
56 CLUTCH CONTROL SWITCH - LEFT
57 CLUTCH CONTROL SWITCH - RIGHT
58 STARTER SWITCH - SELECTOR (L & R)
59 COMPRESSOR INLET SHUT-OFF CONTROL (L & R)
60 OIL DILUTION SWITCH
61 TRIM TAB INDICATOR
62 TRIM TAB SWITCH
63 ARMAMENT MASTER & HEATER SWITCH

64 GUN CONTROL SWITCH
65 GUN SIGHT SWITCH
66 OUTB'D GUN SWITCH
67 INB'D GUN SWITCH
68 ANTI-G SUIT VALVE
69 SEAT CONTROL SWITCH
70 HYDRAULIC HAND PUMP

RIGHT HAND CONSOLE

71 CONTROL AN/ARC-27 UHF
72 CONTROL AN/ARR-2A
73 CONTROL AN/APX-6 IFF
74 B-3 FLIGHT CONTROLER
75 CHANNEL CHART AN/ARC-27
76 AUTO PILOT SELECTOR SWITCH
77 AUTO PILOT MAGNITUDE SWITCH
78 PRE-EJECTION SWITCH
79 DEPRESS. SWITCH - CABIN & FUEL TK.
80 CABIN PRESS. SWITCH
81 PITOT HEATER SWITCH
82 PITOT SELECTOR SWITCH
83 PITOT BLOWOUT VALVE
84 EXTERIOR LIGHT PANEL
85 MAP & DATA CASE
86 CIRCUIT BREAKER PANEL
87 MASTER CONTROL AN/ARC-27

EQUIPMENT

88 ANTENNA & DRIVE ASS'Y. AN/APS-25
89 ANTENNA SERVO AN/APS-25
90 ANTENNA FOLLOW UP AN/APS-25
91 TRANS. & REC'R AN/APS-25
92 SYNCHRONIZER AN/APS-25
93 POWER SUPPLY CI-C AN/APS-25
94 COMPUTER CI-C AN/APS-25
95 COMPUTER BI-C AN/APS-25
96 REC'R & TRANS. AN/ARC-27 UHF
97 RUDDER SERVO UNIT TYPE A-2 E-4AP
98 ELEVON SERVO UNIT TYPE A-2 E-4AP
99 AMPLIFIER TYPE B-6 E-4AP
100 REC'R & TRANS. AN/APX-6
101 RECIEVER AN/ARR-2A
102 GUN SIGHT MK. VI MOD. 1
103 GUN SIGHT AMPLIFIER MK. 53 MOD. 0
104 BALLISTIC COMPUTER CP-63/APG-26
105 BATTERY 24V - 34 AMP. HRS.
106 RADIO ALTIMETER AN/APN-22
107 OXYGEN CYLINDER & VALVE
108 REFRIGERATION UNIT & CABIN PRESS.
109 SERVO CONTROL TYPE O-2 E-4AP
110 AUTO PILOT GYROS
111 PILOT SEAT
112 RELIEF TUBE
113 AC INVERTER
114 AC VOLTAGE REGULATOR
115 DC VOLTAGE REGULATOR
116 CABIN TEMP. & PRESS. CONTROLS
117 CONTROL STICK
118 GUN TRIGGER SWITCH
119 STAND BY COMPASS
120 BULLET PROOF WINDSHIELD
121 CANOPY CONTROL HANDLE
122 FUEL TANK
123 HYDRAULIC FLUID RESERVOIR
124 OIL COOLER

125 OIL TANK
126 BREATHER LINES - ENG.
127 DRAIN LINES - ENG.
128 COOLING DUCT - TURBINE
129 NOSE GEAR
130 RUDDER BOOSTER
131 ELEVON BOOSTER
132 RUDDER PEDALS
133 MIXER
134 SIFTER
135 CANOPY ACTUATOR
136 ENGINE
137 PROPELLER
138 NON-ROTATING SPINNER
139 DUMP TANK
140 TAIL PIPE SHROUD
141 FIN TIP BUMPER
142 ACCUMULATOR
143 MAIN LANDING GEAR
144 GUN CAMERA
145 20MM GUN (4)
146 HOLD-BACK FITTING
147 PITOT HEAD
148 WING TIP BUMPER
149 20MM AMMO. BOX
150 CO_2 CYLINDER
151 FUEL & KEROSENE FILTER
152 OIL QUANTITY GAGE
153 OIL SHUTOFF VALVE

▲ 19

the elimination of the external landing gear and gun fairings would result in a 25 knot increase in maximum speed and a reduction in the time to climb to 35,000 ft to 4.7 minutes. In addition, the outboard gun installation permitted an increase in the diameter of the propeller, resulting in approximately a 2% increase in propeller efficiency which would allow the GA-28B to meet the specified performance requirements.

Automatic Pilot

A control system for both aircraft was proposed which met the control specifications. The design of the system made use of a commercially available autopilot with some modifications. The dynamic analysis of the control system-aircraft loop was carried out both by standard automatic control techniques and by simulation on the Goodyear electronic differential analyzer. From the preliminary analysis of the stability of the airplane without controls in the hovering case, the characteristic equation indicated that it would have been controllable without autopilot if the controls were given constant pilot attention.

Control System Design

The control system had four major divisions:
1. pilot controls
2. autopilot
3. special features
4. airplane controls

The pilot controls consisted of the command selector, the formation stick, the pilot control stick and rudder pedals, the pilot throttle-control, and trim-tab adjustments. The command selector was a switch by which the pilot could select the control system operation mode desired. It was a rotary switch having five different positions which could be selected in any sequence. This was done by declutching the selector knob and moving it to the desired position. When the selector clutch was reengaged, the contacts were snapped to the new position. This feature was necessary since the sequence of modes of operation was not always the same. An interlocking safety device was necessary so that certain switching sequences were prevented. The description of these five modes of control system operation was as follows:

1. The OFF position made the entire autopilot inoperative by disengaging the servo clutches. In this position the pilot control-stick and rudder pedals were in operation through the booster.

2. With the command selector in the HOVERING TO CRUISE position, the servo clutches were engaged and pitch and throttle time programs were initiated to automatically launch the plane and take it through the transition stage to the cruising flight condition. If the airplane was already hovering, the airplane pitch and throttle time programs would not have changed.

3. With the command selector in CRUISE TO HOVERING position, a second pitch and throttle time programmer would have been used and was designed to reverse the procedure used in the HOVERING TO CRUISE mode.

4. When either transition phase was completed, the pilot could switch the command selector to the FORMATION STICK position which allowed the pilot formation stick to be a pitch-and-turn reference and the HEADING KNOB to be a rudder control, except when there was a turn called for by the formation stick— at which time the heading reference was locked out. This allowed the pilot to maneuver in either the vertical or the horizontal positions. It was also possible for the formation stick to have been used in the transition phase, although this was abnormal.

5. In the AUTOPILOT position, the command selector tended to hold the airplane in the heading in which it was flying at the time the AUTOPILOT position was selected. Changes in this heading were made by switching the command selector back to FORMATION STICK position and controlling it to the heading desired with the formation stick.

Ditching

Several aspects of the ditching characteristics of the aircraft are discussed briefly below:

1. If full power was available, a vertical descent was obviously not desirable due to the possibility of the airplane landing on its back once the control surfaces were immersed. The landing velocity for conventional type landings was high, and sinking speed relatively great for the low landing attitude desired to avoid heavy nose impact loads which could be incurred if the tail "dug in" deeply in a high altitude approach.

2. It appeared that a power-on approach in the conventional manner was the optimum method of ditching the vehicles. Pilot technique should have been such as to prevent the propellers from immersing in the water until the airplane was slowed as much as possible. The high location of the cabin shielded by the large chord wing was a favorable

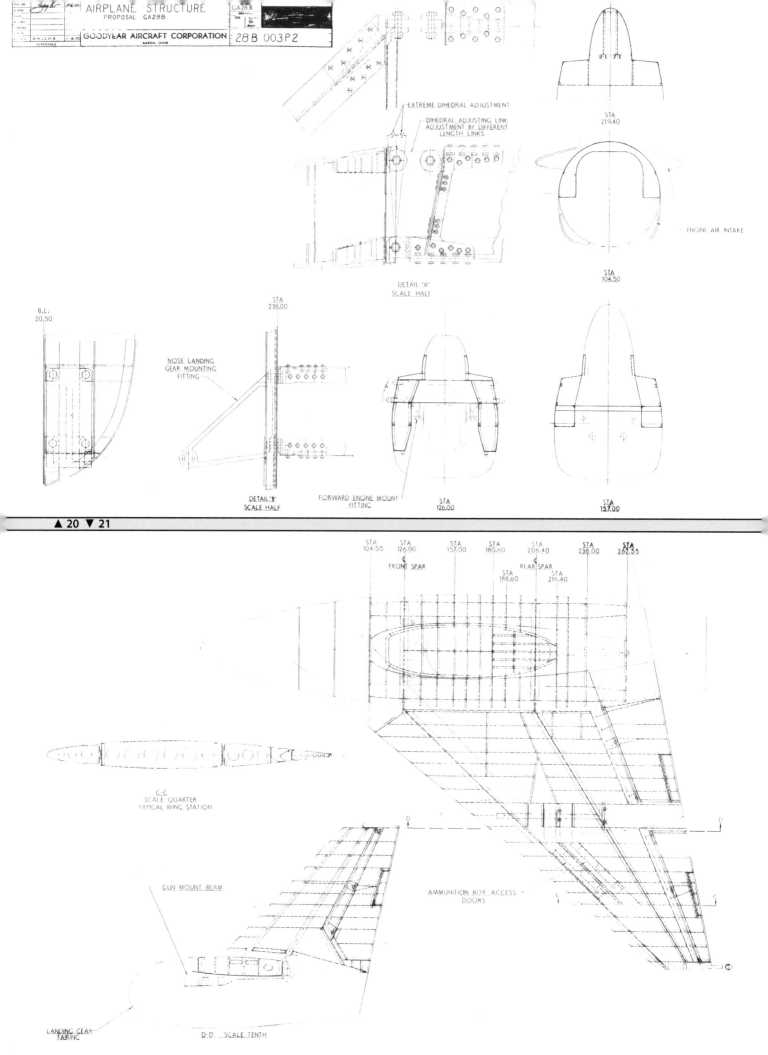

AIRPLANE STRUCTURE
PROPOSAL GA28B

GOODYEAR AIRCRAFT CORPORATION
AKRON, OHIO

GA28B

28B 003P2

EXTREME DIHEDRAL ADJUSTMENT

DIHEDRAL ADJUSTING LINK
ADJUSTMENT BY DIFFERENT
LENGTH LINKS

STA
219.40

ENGINE AIR INTAKE

STA
104.50

DETAIL "A"
SCALE HALF

B.L.
20.50

STA
238.00

NOSE LANDING
GEAR MOUNTING
FITTING

DETAIL "B"
SCALE HALF

FORWARD ENGINE MOUNT
FITTING

STA
126.00

STA
157.00

STA   STA   STA   STA   STA   STA   STA
104.50   126.00   157.00   180.60   206.40   238.00   262.55

FRONT SPAR   REAR SPAR

STA   STA
188.60   219.40

C-C
SCALE QUARTER
TYPICAL WING STATION

GUN MOUNT BEAM

AMMUNITION BOX ACCESS
DOORS

LANDING GEAR
FAIRING

D-D   SCALE TENTH

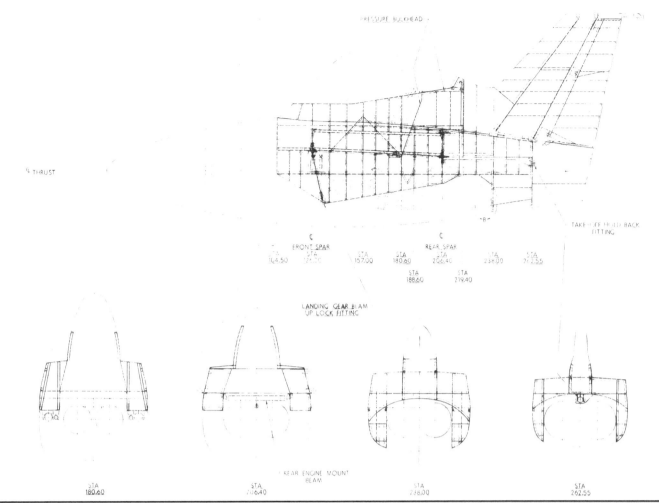

PRESSURE BULKHEAD

THRUST

FRONT SPAR
REAR SPAR

STA
104.50

STA
124.00

STA
157.00

STA
180.60

STA
206.40

STA
238.00

STA
262.55

STA
188.60

STA
219.40

TAKE-OFF HOLD BACK
FITTING

LANDING GEAR BEAM
UP LOCK FITTING

REAR ENGINE MOUNT
BEAM

STA
180.60

STA
206.40

STA
238.00

STA
262.55

▲ 22

feature in that the pilot had sufficient time to escape since the cabin was hinged at the aft end and was easily jettisonable.

3. If no power was available, the landing speed and approach sinking speed would have been in all probability far greater than the airplane structure could withstand.

Cost Proposal

In its Informal Cost Proposal dated December 1, 1950, Goodyear sought to negotiate a mutually acceptable cost plus fixed fee (CPFF) contract with BuAer. Under this arrangement, Goodyear estimated the cost of the GA-28A to be $4,554,300.10 and the GA-28B to be $7,639,287.08; the combined total was $12,193,587.18. Under a fixed price type contract, which Goodyear did not endorse, the cost of the GA-28A was estimated to be $5,692,875.13 and the GA-28B to be $9,549,108.88, for a total of $15,241,984.01. All figures are in 1950's dollars.

The GA-28A would have been ready for flight test approximately 17 months after authority was received to proceed. The second airplane would have been ready for flight test one month later. Goodyear stated that the automatic pilot was the most critical

20-22) Structural blueprint of the GA-28B, which was of conventional stringer and light skin construction with flush joints and riveting throughout. Incorporation of a metal core sandwich material as a means of weight reduction was also considered.

portion of their work in delivering the first prototype. The flight test program for the airplane would have required about 5 months.

The static test article of the GA-28B would have been completed 14 months after the contract was signed. The second airplane would have been ready for flight test 3 months later and the third airplane 3 months after that. The flight test program for the GA-28B would have required about 5 months.

Goodyear recommended that BuAer save time and money by skipping development of the GA-28A prototype and proceeding immediately with construction of the GA-28B. BuAer would soon agree with this advice.

Elimination of the GA-28A

In a letter from Goodyear to BuAer dated December 22, 1950, the company indicated that a stripped-down version of the GA-28B airplane grossing 14,000 lbs at takeoff could be flown on a XT-40-6

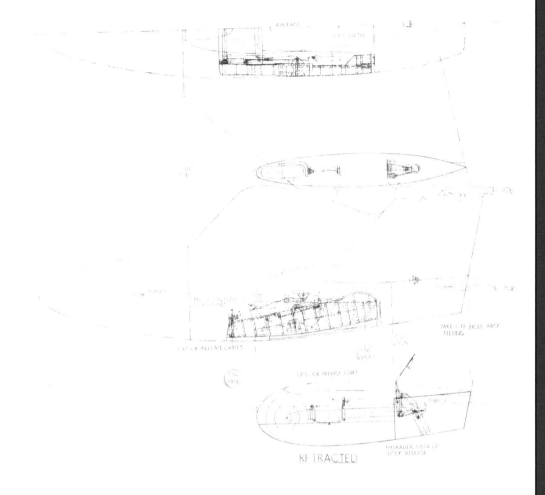

RETRACTED

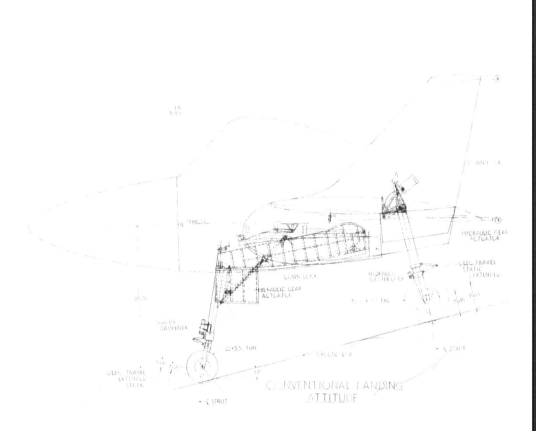

CONVENTIONAL LANDING ATTITUDE

23) A blueprint of the Goodyear GA-28B with the landing gear retracted.

24) The landing gear extended in the conventional landing attitude.

power plant modified for vertical running and still satisfactorily demonstrate transition and adequate maximum speed with endurance approximately the same as for the proposed ¾ scale model GA-28A airplane. This was in accordance with an agreement reached between representatives from Goodyear and BuAer during informal conversations related to the convoy fighter project.

The minimum acceleration of the stripped GA-28B in vertical flight condition with takeoff gross weight of 14,000 lbs was 5 ft/sec². The maximum speed at 35,000 ft at military power (5,500 shaft horsepower) and combat weight of 13,000 lbs was 475 knots.

Why Goodyear Lost

I have not located complete BuAer correspondence regarding the decision behind Goodyear not being awarded a contract in this competition, though I did find a draft table comparing the weights and performance of the various contenders. Goodyear's estimated gross weight for the GA-28B was 17,200 lbs. BuAer analysts estimated it to be more like 18,028 lbs, well over the 16,000 lb gross weight specified in the original OS-122 document. This made it the heaviest of the

25) Drawing of the GA-28B with the landing gear extended in the vertical landing attitude. The complicated rotating nose gear assembly must be among the strangest ever contemplated for an aircraft. The 180° rotation of the main gear is also noteworthy.

26) Late in the development of their proposal, Goodyear drew up an alternate main gear arrangement where the outboard pods were deleted and the gear retracted inwards towards the fuselage.

proposals submitted to the convoy fighter competition, and shows that there was a definite penalty in eliminating the auxiliary handling gear and incorporating the landing gear within the aircraft. Excess weight is a more serious problem for a VTOL aircraft than a conventional aircraft, making the already challenging take-offs and landings even more hazardous.

One must note that Goodyear had less experience building aircraft than its competitors. While it did a satisfactory job developing the FG-1 and F2G-1 variants of the Corsair fighter during WW II, it was primarily known for producing blimps, tires and other rubber products. The convoy fighter program was an unconventional and technically challenging program, and BuAer may have felt that it was beyond the company's capabilities.

Finally, it is worth pointing out that Convair also proposed a delta wing design and had more expertise with the configuration, having already flown the XF-92A on April 1, 1948. If the

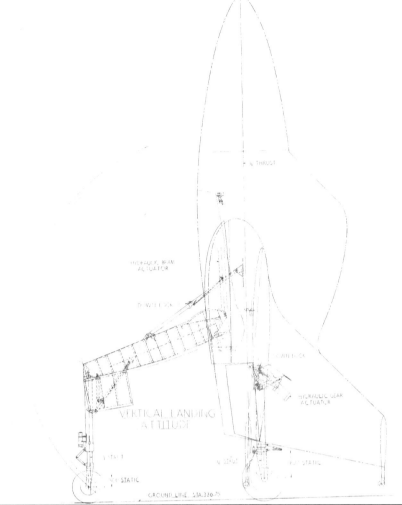

▲ 25 ▼ 26

ALTERNATE MAIN LANDING GEAR

GOODYEAR AIRCRAFT CORPORATION
AKRON, OHIO

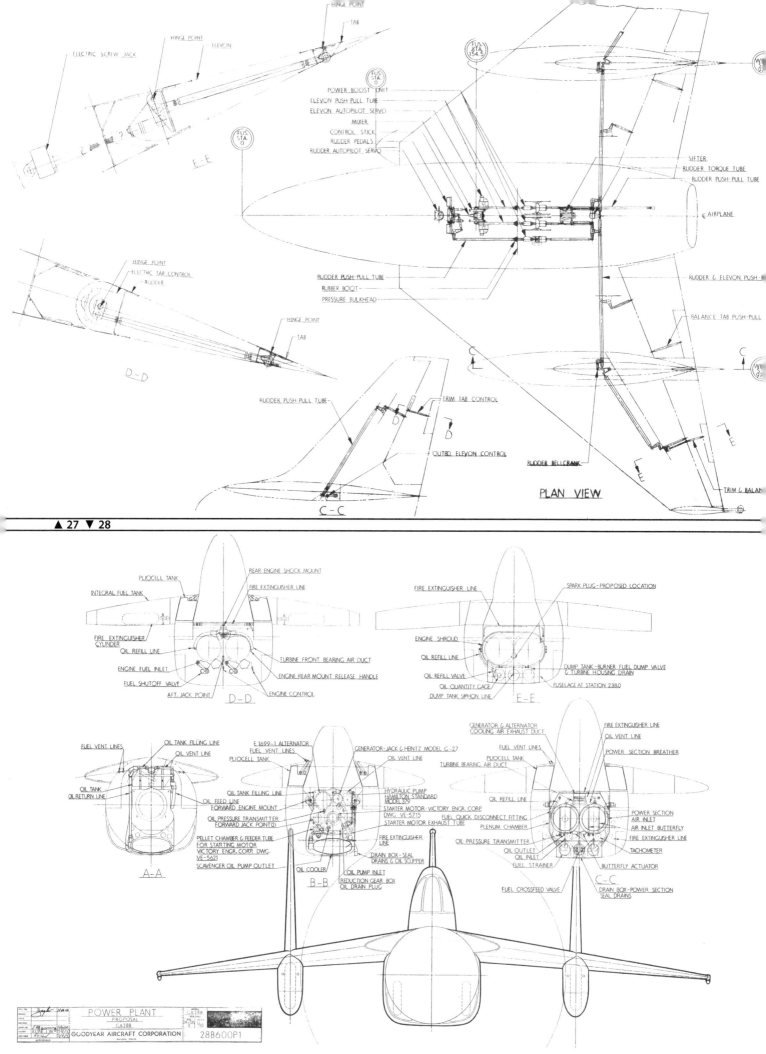

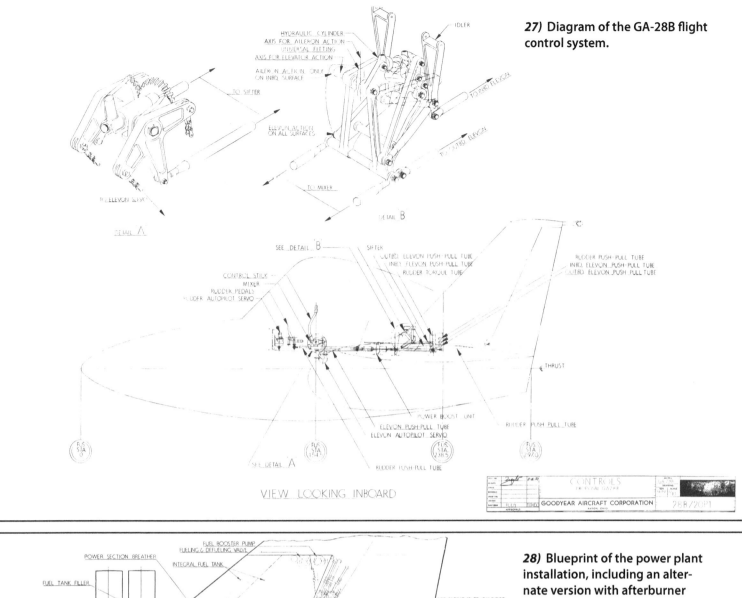

27) Diagram of the GA-28B flight control system.

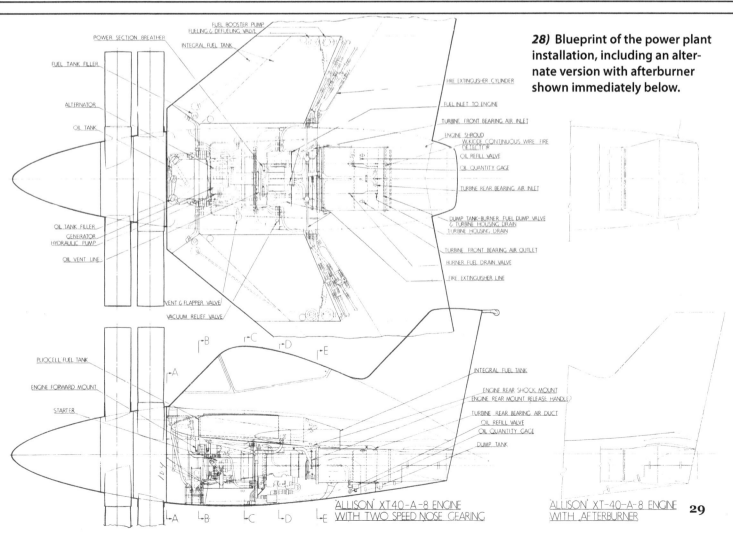

28) Blueprint of the power plant installation, including an alternate version with afterburner shown immediately below.

ALLISON XT-40-A-8 ENGINE WITH TWO SPEED NOSE GEARING

ALLISON XT-40-A-8 ENGINE WITH AFTERBURNER

29

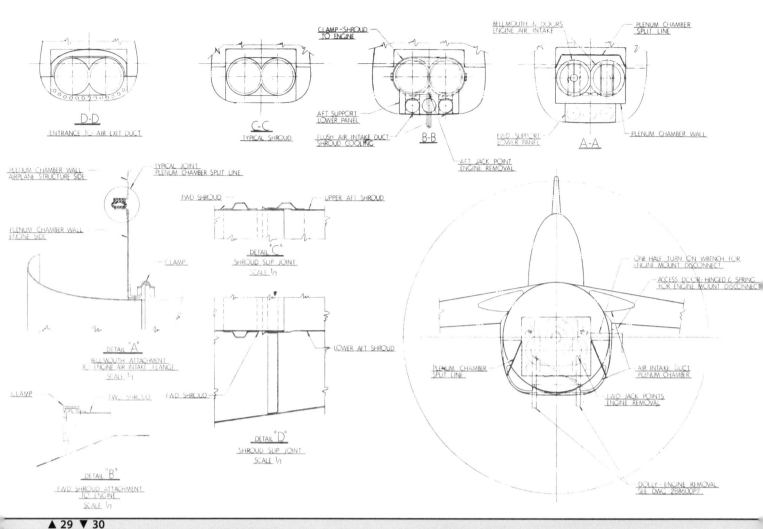

D-D
ENTRANCE TO AIR EXIT DUCT

C-C
TYPICAL SHROUD

B-B

A-A

CLAMP-SHROUD TO ENGINE

AFT SUPPORT LOWER PANEL

FLUSH AIR INTAKE DUCT SHROUD COOLING

BELLMOUTH & DOORS ENGINE AIR INTAKE

PLENUM CHAMBER SPLIT LINE

FWD SUPPORT LOWER PANEL

PLENUM CHAMBER WALL

AFT JACK POINT ENGINE REMOVAL

PLENUM CHAMBER WALL AIRPLANE STRUCTURE SIDE

TYPICAL JOINT PLENUM CHAMBER SPLIT LINE

FWD SHROUD

UPPER AFT SHROUD

PLENUM CHAMBER WALL ENGINE SIDE

DETAIL "C"
SHROUD SLIP JOINT
SCALE 1/1

CLAMP

DETAIL "A"
BELLMOUTH ATTACHMENT TO ENGINE AIR INTAKE FLANGE
SCALE 1/1

LOWER AFT SHROUD

CLAMP

FWD SHROUD

FWD SHROUD

DETAIL "B"
FWD SHROUD ATTACHMENT TO ENGINE
SCALE 1/1

DETAIL "D"
SHROUD SLIP JOINT
SCALE 1/1

ONE HALF TURN ON WRENCH FOR ENGINE MOUNT DISCONNECT

ACCESS DOOR-HINGED & SPRING FOR ENGINE MOUNT DISCONNECT

PLENUM CHAMBER SPLIT LINE

AIR INTAKE DUCT PLENUM CHAMBER

FWD JACK POINTS ENGINE REMOVAL

DOLLY- ENGINE REMOVAL SEE DWG 28B600P7

ENGINE ACCESSABILITY & REMOVAL
PROPOSAL
GA-28B
GOODYEAR AIRCRAFT CORPORATION
AKRON, OHIO
28B600P6

"ALLISON" XT40-A-8 ENGINE WITH AFTERBURNER

CLAMP FOR AFTERBURNER REMOVAL

AFT PANEL REMOVABLE AFTERBURNER ACCESS & ENGINE REMOVAL

AIR EXIT DUCT
OIL COOLING
GENERATOR COOLING
ALTERNATOR COOLING
TURBINE BEARING COOLING
ACCESSORY COMPARTMENT COOLING

AFTERBURNER

FLUSH TYPE LATCH

NOTE
FLUID LINES, ELECTRICAL LINES & ENGINE CONTROLS TO CONNECT OR DISCONNECT AUTOMATICALLY BY UTILIZING ENGINE VERTICAL MOVEMENT THRU ONE INCH OF GUIDE TRAVEL INCORPORATED IN ENGINE MOUNT FITTINGS (SEE DWG 28B600P7)

29) Engine accessability and removal diagram for the Goodyear GA-28B.

30) Engine accessability and removal diagram for the afterburner-equipped version of the fighter.

31) Perspective drawing of the power plant quick change unit.

Navy wanted to evaluate a delta wing design, Convair was the better choice from a risk standpoint.

Perhaps it wasn't such a bad thing for Goodyear to lose the competition, as testing of the Convair XFY-1 and Lockheed XFV-1 revealed the turboprop tailsitter fighter concept to be seriously flawed, with neither going beyond the prototype stage. There is scant evidence that the GA-28B would have done any better, though watching it attempt both vertical and horizontal takeoffs and landings would have been interesting.

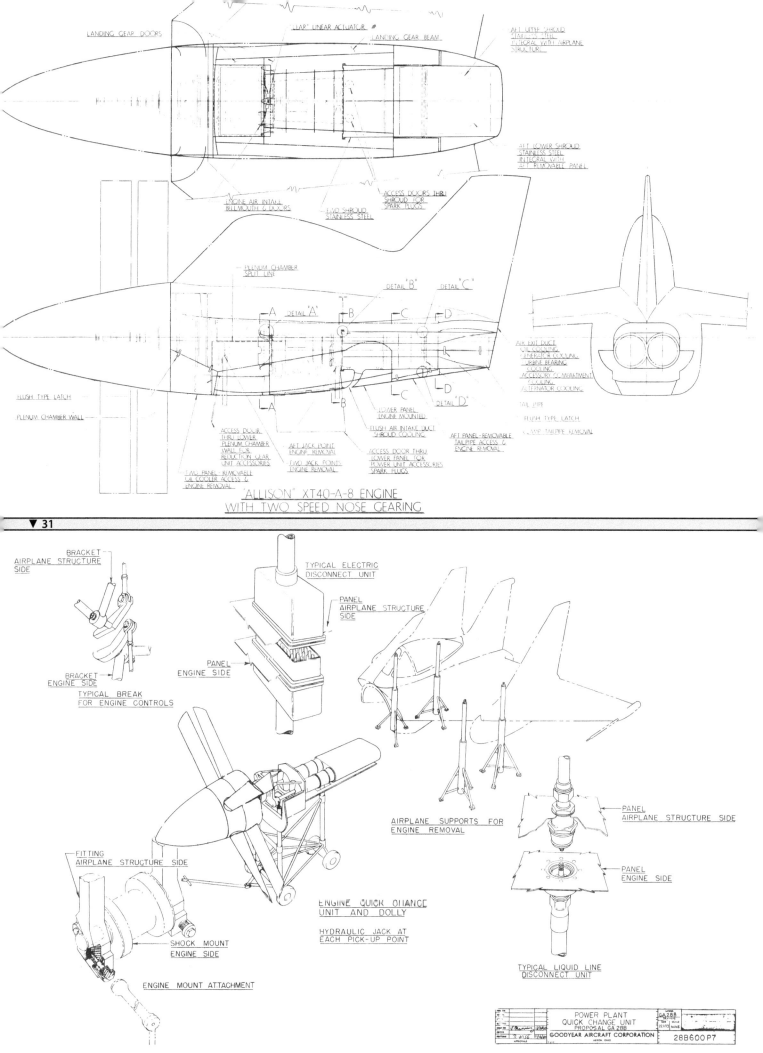

LANDING GEAR DOORS

"GEAR" LINEAR ACTUATOR

LANDING GEAR BEAM

AFT UPPER SHROUD
STAINLESS STEEL
INTEGRAL WITH AIRPLANE
STRUCTURE

AFT LOWER SHROUD
STAINLESS STEEL
INTEGRAL WITH
AFT REMOVABLE PANEL

ENGINE AIR INTAKE
BELLMOUTH & DOORS

FWD SHROUD
STAINLESS STEEL

ACCESS DOORS THRU
SHROUD FOR
SPARK PLUGS

PLENUM CHAMBER
SPLIT LINE

DETAIL "B"   DETAIL "C"

DETAIL "A"

A   B   C   D

AIR EXIT DUCT
OIL COOLING
GENERATOR COOLING
TURBINE BEARING
COOLING
ACCESSORY COMPARTMENT
COOLING
ALTERNATOR COOLING

FLUSH TYPE LATCH

PLENUM CHAMBER WALL

C   D

DETAIL "D"

A   B   C

LOWER PANEL
ENGINE MOUNTED

TAIL PIPE

FLUSH TYPE LATCH

FLAME TAILPIPE REMOVAL

ACCESS DOOR
THRU LOWER
PLENUM CHAMBER
WALL FOR
REDUCTION GEAR
UNIT ACCESSORIES

AFT JACK POINT
ENGINE REMOVAL

FWD JACK POINT
ENGINE REMOVAL

FLUSH AIR INTAKE DUCT
SHROUD COOLING

ACCESS DOOR THRU
LOWER PANEL FOR
POWER UNIT ACCESSORIES
SPARK PLUGS

AFT PANEL-REMOVABLE
TAILPIPE ACCESS &
ENGINE REMOVAL

FWD PANEL - REMOVABLE
OIL COOLER ACCESS &
ENGINE REMOVAL

"ALLISON" XT40-A-8 ENGINE
WITH TWO SPEED NOSE GEARING

BRACKET
AIRPLANE STRUCTURE
SIDE

TYPICAL ELECTRIC
DISCONNECT UNIT

PANEL
AIRPLANE STRUCTURE
SIDE

PANEL
ENGINE SIDE

BRACKET
ENGINE SIDE

TYPICAL BREAK
FOR ENGINE CONTROLS

AIRPLANE SUPPORTS FOR
ENGINE REMOVAL

PANEL
AIRPLANE STRUCTURE SIDE

FITTING
AIRPLANE STRUCTURE SIDE

SHOCK MOUNT
ENGINE SIDE

ENGINE MOUNT ATTACHMENT

PANEL
ENGINE SIDE

ENGINE QUICK CHANGE
UNIT AND DOLLY

HYDRAULIC JACK AT
EACH PICK-UP POINT

TYPICAL LIQUID LINE
DISCONNECT UNIT

POWER PLANT
QUICK CHANGE UNIT
PROPOSAL GA 28B

GOODYEAR AIRCRAFT CORPORATION
AKRON, OHIO

28B600 P7

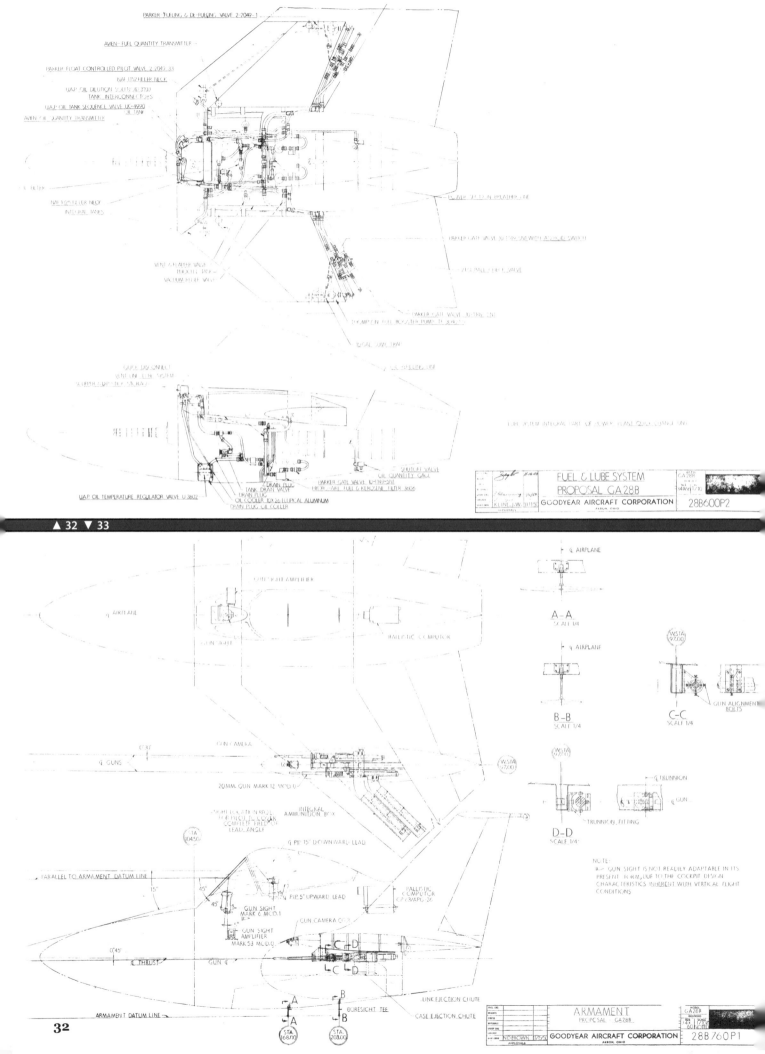

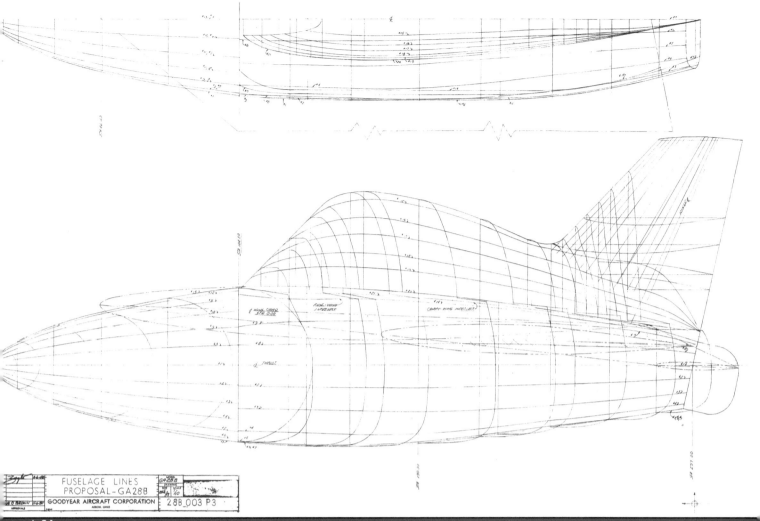

FUSELAGE LINES
PROPOSAL-GA28B
GOODYEAR AIRCRAFT CORPORATION
AKRON, OHIO

28B_003 P3

I am developing 1/72 scale limited edition resin kits of both the GA-28A and GA-28B; if interested, please sign up online at *retromechanix.com/surveys* to receive news of their availability.

32) Blueprint of the GA-28B's fuel and lubrication system.

33) The GA-28B was armed with four 20 mm Mark 12 Mod. 0 cannons, two in each wing pod.

34) The fuselage loft lines of the GA-28B.

Other Publications by Jared A. Zichek

The American Aerospace Archive Magazine
Available at magcloud.com/user/jaredzichek

1. Martin JRM Mars Flying Boat: Commercial Projects of 1944 Reproduction of a beautiful full color brochure for a civilian version of the world's largest flying boat; 36 pp. **Print $9.95/Digital $3.95**

2. North American FJ-5 Fighter: A Navalized Derivative of the F-107A Five wind tunnel model photos and 28 drawings of North American's unusual 1955 proposal; 36 pp. **Print $9.95/Digital $3.95**

3. The B-52 Competition of 1946...and Dark Horses from Douglas, 1947-1950 Seventy-seven rare images of early postwar strategic bomber projects; 60 pp. **Print $14.95/Digital $5.95**

4. McDonnell Naval Jet Fighters: Selected Proposals and Mock-up Reports, 1945-1957 97 photos and drawings of early postwar jet fighter proposals & prototypes; 60 pp. **Print $14.95/Digital $5.95**

5. Mother Ships, Parasites and More: Selected USAF Strategic Bomber, XC Heavy Transport and FICON Studies, 1945-1954 Composite aircraft projects; 258 illos; 204 pp. **Print $49.95/Digital $9.95**

Books from Schiffer Publishing
Available from Amazon.com & other booksellers

The Boeing XF8B-1 Fighter: Last of the Line Hundreds of rare photos, drawings, artist's impressions and manual extracts covering Boeing's last piston engine fighter; 376 pp. **$45.59**

Secret Aerospace Projects of the U.S. Navy: The Incredible Attack Aircraft of the USS United States, 1948-1949 Hundreds of rare photos and drawings; 232 pp. **$45.81**

Websites

RETRO MECHANIX
Yesterday's Wings of Tomorrow

Retromechanix.com Features hundreds of rare high resolution images and reports covering U.S. prototype and project aircraft from the 1930s through the 1950s. Many free and and low cost digital downloads available!

Lightning Source UK Ltd.
Milton Keynes UK
UKHW050415220222
399034UK00002B/137